#Pride

Championing LGBTQ Rights

Rebecca Felix

Abdo & Daughters

An Imprint of Abdo Publishing
abdobooks.com

abdobooks.com

Published by Abdo Publishing, a division of ABDO, PO Box 398166, Minneapolis, Minnesota 55439. Copyright © 2020 by Abdo Consulting Group, Inc. International copyrights reserved in all countries. No part of this book may be reproduced in any form without written permission from the publisher. Abdo & Daughters™ is a trademark and logo of Abdo Publishing.

Printed in the United States of America, North Mankato, Minnesota
052019
092019

THIS BOOK CONTAINS
RECYCLED MATERIALS

Design: Aruna Rangarajan, Mighty Media, Inc.
Production: Mighty Media, Inc.
Editor: Liz Salzmann
Cover Photographs: Shutterstock
Interior Photographs: Design elements, Shutterstock; AP Images, pp. 8, 15, 29 (bottom); Flickr, pp. 7, 28 (bottom); Getty Images, pp. 13, 19; Shutterstock, pp. 3, 4–5, 10–11, 17, 22, 25, 26–27, 28 (top), 29 (top right), 29 (top left); Wikimedia Commons, p. 21

Library of Congress Control Number: 2018966468

Publisher's Cataloging-in-Publication Data
Names: Felix, Rebecca, author.
Title: #Pride: championing LGBTQ rights / by Rebecca Felix
Other title: Championing LGBTQ rights
Description: Minneapolis, Minnesota : Abdo Publishing, 2020 | Series: #Movements | Includes online resources and index.
Identifiers: ISBN 9781532119330 (lib. bdg.) | ISBN 9781532173790 (ebook)
Subjects: LCSH: Sexual minority community--Juvenile literature. | Equality--United States--Juvenile literature. | Sexual orientation discrimination--Juvenile literature. | Protest movements--Juvenile literature.
Classification: DDC 305.38--dc23

CONTENTS

#Pride. 4

LGBTQ Rights History 6

The Stonewall Riots. 10

Pride Begins. 12

Rights & Rainbows 14

Media Impact 16

Anti-LGBTQ Crime 18

Making History & Hashtags 20

Is Pride Just a Party?. 24

Modern Pride. 26

Timeline 28

Glossary. 30

Online Resources 31

Index. 32

What is pride? It can be respect for something, someone, or yourself. It can also be happiness or excitement about something you have accomplished. Nearly 50 years ago, pride took on another meaning. It came to represent a movement in support of equal treatment for LGBTQ people.

The Pride movement started with a riot against injustice. It grew into a march, a series of events, and finally, a hashtag. #Pride is used to label social media posts related to all of these things. It is meant to spread pride in being LGBTQ. It is also meant to make others aware of the LGBTQ community's ongoing fight for equal rights.

Pride events take place globally each June. But the hashtag #Pride is seen in online posts daily. People use the hashtag to share encouragement, demand equality, and celebrate being true to one's identity.

LET'S TALK TERMS

Each letter in LGBTQ represents a sexual identity. Lesbians are women attracted to other women. Gay men are attracted to other men. Bisexual people are attracted to both sexes. Transgender and transsexual people identify as a gender other than the one they were born as. Queer is a term that can be used for anyone who is not heterosexual.

Rainbow colors and flags are often symbols for Pride.

Pride is meant for anyone who does not identify as heterosexual. But the movement includes and accepts anyone who wants to support LGBTQ people. Today, this includes the majority of Americans. But this general acceptance is new in the span of LBGTQ history. For decades, this community faced discrimination, hatred, and violence.

Today, the LGBTQ rights movement thrives with visibility and support. But the LGBTQ community only won acceptance by fighting for it. The Pride movement grew from outrage over years of discrimination, abuse, and criminalization of LGBTQ people.

Historically, religion has played a large role in LGBTQ oppression. Christianity and some other world religions often condemn homosexuality. These beliefs have also influenced the attitudes that non-religious people have about the LGBTQ community.

As a whole, the US public disapproved of homosexuality for centuries. Some people even openly expressed hatred of LGBTQ people. Certain sexual relations associated with homosexuality were illegal until 2003. Because of this general disapproval, few LGBTQ Americans were open about their sexual identities.

However, some people saw the condemnation of homosexuality as a human rights issue. In 1924, Henry Gerber founded the Society for Human Rights. It is the first official gay rights organization in the United States.

In 1948, well-known US scientist Alfred Kinsey published a book about human sexuality. He included explorations of non-heterosexuality. The book gave the LGBTQ community more visibility. This gave many people the courage to come out.

Alfred Kinsey (*center*) founded the Institute for Sex Research at Indiana University. Today it is called the Kinsey Institute for Sex, Gender, and Reproduction.

Frank Kameny was fired from his government job for being gay. He then became a gay rights activist. He helped organize the first gay rights march in Philadelphia in 1965.

The greater visibility of LGBTQ lifestyles angered opponents of gay rights, including many in the psychological profession. The American Psychiatric Association considered homosexuality to be a mental disease.

Government officials also reacted negatively. Openly gay men were banned from the US military. Police officers began raiding known gay bars to arrest patrons.

In 1953, new laws targeted homosexual citizens. President Dwight D. Eisenhower signed an order making it illegal for them to work for the US government. Some Americans considered this policy a form of oppression and harassment. In response, an opposing movement of support grew in the LGBTQ community. Activists formed gay rights groups and sought equality. But the push and pull of support for and against homosexuality would continue for decades.

In the 1960s, the LGBTQ rights movement made progress. In 1961, Illinois became the first state to decriminalize sexual relations associated with homosexuality. And in 1965, about 40 activists gathered in Philadelphia, Pennsylvania. They marched silently in front of Independence Hall, holding signs demanding equal treatment for LGBTQ citizens. This was the first US LGBTQ rights demonstration. But it was a much more turbulent gathering four years later that started the gay rights movement in a memorable way.

In 1969, sexual relations between gay people were still illegal in New York City. The city's LGBTQ residents were often harassed. So, they created places where they felt safe to gather. One of these places was the Stonewall Inn.

The New York police knew the Stonewall Inn was a meeting place for LGBTQ people. They often went there to make sure its patrons weren't breaking any laws. One of these visits was early in the morning of June 28, 1969.

Nine officers arrived at the Stonewall Inn and used force to evacuate the bar's 200 patrons. At the time, there was a New York City law against dressing inappropriately for one's gender. The officers arrested several people for breaking this law.

New York City's LGBTQ community was accustomed to similar raids and arrests. Usually, its members scattered after such a scene. But this time, they didn't. They got angry about being continually harassed and oppressed. The crowd outside the bar became aggressive toward the police. This turned into a riot. More people arrived, swelling the crowd to about 400 people.

The officers retreated into the Stonewall Inn to escape the rioters. Then, some of the rioters set the bar on fire. Soon, police backup arrived.

In June 2016, President Barack Obama established the Stonewall National Monument. It is in New York City, across the street from the Stonewall Inn.

But the rioting continued for several days. No one was killed, but a number of police officers and community members were injured. In the end, the Stonewall Riots had a profound, lasting impact.

Historians credit the Stonewall Riots for making members of the LGBTQ community aware of their power in uniting for a common cause. It marked the beginning of the modern US LGBTQ rights movement. Members of the LGBTQ community in New York City wanted to commemorate the one-year anniversary of the Stonewall Riots. Activists Craig Rodwell and Brenda Howard formed a committee to plan a march to be held on the last Saturday in June.

Committee member L. Craig Schoonmaker suggested calling the event "Gay Pride." The rest of the committee liked Shoonmaker's idea. The LGBTQ pride movement was born. In addition to Gay Pride, the movement was also often called Gay Freedom or Gay Liberation.

The first Gay Pride March took place on June 28, 1970. The main march was in New York City. A few other US cities also held marches that day. Gay pride events, often simply called Pride, have been held every year since. As more Americans participated in Pride, activists worked to develop the movement's mission.

LET'S TALK TERMS

The terms represented by LGBTQ can carry different meanings to different people. It is considered most respectful to ask how an individual identifies.

The 1970 Gay Pride March was called Christopher Street Liberation Day March. Some marchers carried "Mattachine" signs. This was for the Mattachine Society, an early American gay rights organization.

Rights & Rainbows

The LGBTQ rights movement developed several goals. It fought to end harassment of LGBTQ people ranging from general public disapproval to violent hate crimes. Other goals included ending military and employment discrimination against LGBTQ people and gaining the right to marry someone of the same sex. In 1973, Maryland became the first state to pass a law denying people of the same sex the right to get married. Over the next 20 years, most other US states followed suit.

Above all, the LGBTQ rights movement sought to protect the rights of all persons who identify as something other than heterosexual. In 1978, the community created a symbol to represent its many identities.

California artist Gilbert Baker was hired to design a flag for the 1978 San Francisco Gay Freedom Day Parade march. Baker chose a rainbow pattern. He felt its many colors represented the many different members of the LGBTQ community. The rainbow flag was adopted as the movement's symbol. The rainbow flag and rainbow colors soon became the visual theme of LGBTQ rights and of Pride.

June Pride events remained the LGBTQ community's main celebratory events and forms of protest. By 1984, Pride events took place in many US cities and in some other countries. Later that decade, the birth of the internet helped further connect LGBTQ communities around the world.

THE FACE OF #PRIDE

Gilbert Baker

Gilbert Baker was an LGBTQ activist, designer, and gay man. He designed the first rainbow flags that went on to represent the LBGTQ Pride movement around the world. Baker himself became a face of the movement.

In 1994, Baker set a world record when he created a huge rainbow flag for that year's Pride. It was one mile (1.6 km) long. In 2003, he broke that record by creating a rainbow flag that was 1.25 miles (2.0 km) long! Baker was often asked to be grand marshal of Pride parades around the world.

In 2015, the New York City Museum of Modern Art added one of Baker's rainbow flags to its permanent design collection. In 2016, Baker presented President Barack Obama with one of these flags at the White House. The president had invited Baker there to commemorate LGBT Pride Month. Baker died the next year. But his flag lives on as the symbol of the movement he supported his entire life.

Media Impact

The internet was created in the mid-1980s and was offered in limited locations. By 1991, it had spread around the world. From the internet's earliest years, members of the LGBTQ community created newsgroups, chat rooms, and other online spaces. These spaces provided opportunities for LGBTQ people to openly express themselves.

In the 1990s, more LGBTQ people were coming out publicly than ever before. But there was still a general disapproval of LGBTQ lifestyles. Many LGBTQ people were still too scared or worried to come out. They were afraid of facing harassment or discrimination. The internet created safe spaces for people to come out anonymously. They could connect privately with other LGBTQ people and discuss their feelings and struggles.

The internet became a significant tool for strengthening Pride and the LGBTQ rights movement. In 1997, another form of media gave the LGBTQ community greater visibility. By this time, television had been a major part of US entertainment for decades. But there had never been a national show featuring a main character who was openly LGBTQ.

In April 1997, actress Ellen DeGeneres's character came out as a lesbian on her popular TV show, *Ellen*. DeGeneres also came out in real life. Her coming out was the beginning of an era of celebrity support of LGBTQ rights.

More than 40 million viewers tuned in to watch DeGeneres's "coming out" episode of *Ellen* in 1997.

17

Anti-LGBTQ Crime

In the late 1990s, the media continued to give Pride and LGBTQ rights greater visibility. In 1998, news of a violent hate crime spread around the world in print, on television, and online. That October, a young man was beaten to death because of his sexuality.

Matthew Shepard was an openly gay 21-year-old living in Wyoming. Two men attacked Shepard because he was gay. They tied him to a fence. They left him there, badly injured. Shepard wasn't found for 18 hours. He later died from his injuries.

Shepard's death caused a new wave of protest in the LGBTQ community. LGBTQ rights advocates marched and protested around the nation. US celebrities and politicians spoke out against anti-gay violence. The next year, Wyoming lawmakers proposed extending a law against hate crimes to include anti-LGBTQ crimes. But when put to a vote in the state House of Representatives, the law did not pass.

Ending anti-LGBTQ violence remained a focus of Pride. In 2009, their efforts paid off on a national scale. That year, a US law named in honor of Shepard went into effect. It expanded punishable hate crimes to include those based on a person's sexuality or gender identity.

Thousands of people attended memorials and protests for Shepard.

MATTHEW SHEPARD

killed by HOMOPHOBIA

19

The Matthew Shepard Act and other LGBTQ successes in the 2000s were helped by the debut of several social media websites. These included Facebook, Twitter, Instagram, and YouTube. These sites gave the LGBTQ community new platforms to increase awareness and support.

Historians cite social media as a key reason LGBTQ acceptance increased in the 2000s. After Twitter invented hashtags in 2007, social media users started using the hashtag #Pride in many kinds of posts. These posts were about being LGBTQ, celebrating Pride events, and supporting LGBTQ rights. Over time, public acceptance of LGBTQ lifestyles increased. Eventually, support of LGBTQ rights started to outweigh disapproval.

TAGGED

"The first #pride flag flew in 1978. Today we understand what it really means. #LoveWins"
—media corporation Google
(@Google, Twitter)

The 2000s saw several law changes related to LGBTQ rights. In April 2000, Vermont became the first state to legalize same sex civil unions. In 2003, the US Supreme Court ruled that laws banning sexual relations associated with homosexuality were unconstitutional. The next year, Massachusetts became the first state to legalize same-sex marriages.

Don't Ask, Don't Tell was a policy that required people in the military not to disclose their sexual orientation. The policy was repealed in 2011 by President Barack Obama.

On the night of the same-sex marriage ruling, the White House was lit with rainbow colors to acknowledge the achievement of the gay rights movement.

Many other states legalized these unions in the following years. In 2011, the ban on openly LGBTQ people serving in the US military was ended.

In 2015, the LGBTQ focus returned to marriage rights. On June 26, the Supreme Court ruled same-sex marriages legal in all 50 states. The ruling was announced 46 years after the Stonewall Riots. Around the nation, crowds gathered to celebrate. People also celebrated on social media.

Millions of #Pride posts filled social media sites. Within one hour of the ruling, there were 10.1 million Facebook interactions relating to the topic. Within three hours, there had been 6.2 million tweets about it! People around the nation posted selfies and celebratory messages. Many added other hashtags, such as #LoveIsLove, #MarriageEquality, and #LoveWins. Twitter created custom emojis that added rainbows to posts that included #LoveWins or #Pride.

LGBTQ people were not the only ones to post these hashtags. Many heterosexual supporters also posted in celebration of the ruling. These supporters included people with LGBTQ family members, friends, and coworkers. They also included advocates for human rights. Many businesses also posted in support of the ruling.

Marriage equality was a popular theme at the 2015 Pride events. The related hashtags were on signs, flags, and more. The ruling lent an especially celebratory tone to that year's festivals.

TAGGED

"J-E-L-L-O is for everyone. So is L-O-V-E. #DecisionDay #Pride"
—Jell-O dessert food brand (@JELLO, Twitter)

Is Pride Just a Party?

Pride has expanded from its origins. What began as a yearly, one-day march has stretched into a weekend festival. In some places, it is a monthlong series of events. The celebratory aspect of being openly LGBTQ has also intensified.

LGBTQ people have historically felt pressure from society to hide their sexuality. To some, Pride is a chance to freely express it. But others have said this expression sometimes goes too far and becomes obscene.

Some members of the LGBTQ community have expressed concern that Pride is geared toward white gay men who use the festival to meet one another. Critics have said these types of Pride events do not give equal representation to the many members of the LGBTQ community.

Critics have also worried that the flashy displays at some Pride events overshadow the political statements that Pride was established to make. Losing sight of the political statements behind Pride has been its main criticism. But events in 2016 and 2017 returned attention to the movement's original motives.

TAGGED

"Happy #PRIDE month. I see you and I love you"
—singer Katy Perry (@katyperry, Twitter)

Istanbul, Turkey, is one of many cities outside the US that have held Pride events in recent years.

On June 12, 2016, an American man entered a gay bar in Orlando, Florida. He shot and killed 49 people and wounded 53 more. It was the deadliest attack against LGBTQ people in history.

In 2017, Donald Trump became president of the United States. Many LGBTQ groups felt Trump and his administration were anti-LGBTQ and would undo Pride's progress. In July of that year, Trump announced a ban on transgender people serving in the US military. A federal court shut down this proposal. However, in January 2019, a US court ruled that in some circumstances transgender people could be banned from the military.

The Orlando shooting and Trump's policies brought the original motives behind Pride back into focus. LGBTQ groups united to fight for equal rights and end violence against their community. Many media outlets and advocates wondered if these recent attacks against LGBTQ people marked a permanent return of Pride to its root causes.

TAGGED

"Unspeakable. So much suffering today. My heart goes out to the families of the victims in Orlando. #Pride"
—actress Mindy Kaling
(@mindykaling, Twitter)

People around the world held candlelight memorials and other events in memory of those killed in the Orlando attack.

The Pride movement has come a long way. But modern events prove it still has a long way to go. In whatever ways the movement transforms in the future, #Pride will capture it one post at a time.

TIMELINE

Henry Gerber founds the Society for Human Rights.

1924

Illinois becomes the first state to decriminalize sexual acts associated with homosexuality.

1961

The Stonewall Riots begin when police raid a gay bar in New York City. These events become the base upon which the LGBTQ Pride movement is built.

June 28, 1969

1948

Alfred Kinsey publishes a book about human sexuality, which gives the LGBTQ community greater visibility.

1965

Activists in Philadelphia, Pennsylvania, gather to demand equal rights for LGBTQ people.

1970

The term "gay pride" is coined. The first Gay Pride March occurs on June 28 to commemorate the Stonewall Riots.

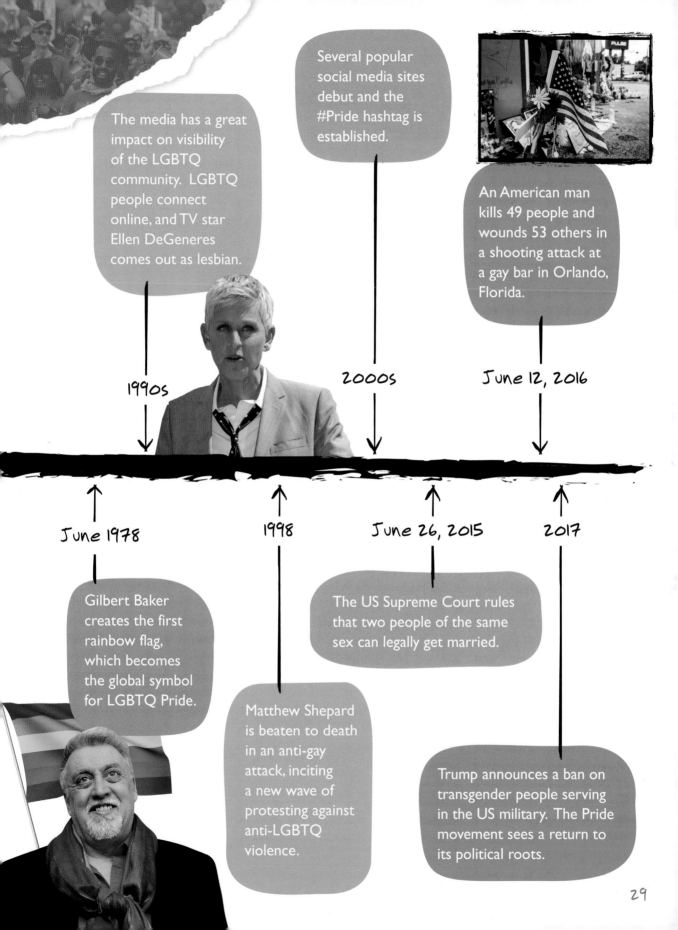

The media has a great impact on visibility of the LGBTQ community. LGBTQ people connect online, and TV star Ellen DeGeneres comes out as lesbian.

Several popular social media sites debut and the #Pride hashtag is established.

An American man kills 49 people and wounds 53 others in a shooting attack at a gay bar in Orlando, Florida.

1990s

2000s

June 12, 2016

June 1978

1998

June 26, 2015

2017

Gilbert Baker creates the first rainbow flag, which becomes the global symbol for LGBTQ Pride.

The US Supreme Court rules that two people of the same sex can legally get married.

Matthew Shepard is beaten to death in an anti-gay attack, inciting a new wave of protesting against anti-LGBTQ violence.

Trump announces a ban on transgender people serving in the US military. The Pride movement sees a return to its political roots.

29

GLOSSARY

activist—a person who takes direct action in support of or in opposition to an issue that causes disagreement.

advocate—a person who defends or supports a cause.

anniversary—the date of a special event that is often celebrated each year.

anonymously—without giving your name.

commemorate—to serve as a memorial of something.

criminalize—to make something illegal.

decriminalize—to make something legal.

discrimination—unfair treatment, often based on race, religion, or gender.

emoji—a small symbol or picture that can be typed in an email, a text, or an online post.

gay bar—a bar that has mostly LGBTQ customers.

gender—the behaviors, characteristics, and qualities most often associated with either the male or female sex.

harass—to annoy or bother someone again and again. This behavior is called harassment.

hashtag—a word or phrase used in social media posts, such as tweets, that starts with the symbol # and that briefly indicates what the post is about.

heterosexual—attracted to people of a different sex than yours.

homosexual—attracted to people of the same sex as yours.

inappropriate—not suitable, fitting, or proper.

obscene—offensive or disgusting.

participate—to take part or share in something.

social media—websites or smartphone apps that provide information and entertainment and allow people to communicate with each other. Facebook and Twitter are examples of social media.

Supreme Court—the highest, most powerful court in the United States.

unconstitutional—something that goes against the laws of a constitution.

ONLINE RESOURCES

Booklinks
NONFICTION NETWORK
FREE! ONLINE NONFICTION RESOURCES

To learn more about #Pride, please visit **abdobooklinks.com** or scan this QR code. These links are routinely monitored and updated to provide the most current information available.

INDEX

American Psychiatric Association, 9
anti-LGBTQ laws, 9, 10, 14, 26

Baker, Gilbert, 14, 15

Christianity, 6

DeGeneres, Ellen, 16

Eisenhower, Dwight D., 9
Ellen, 16

Florida, 26

Gerber, Henry, 6

Howard, Brenda, 12

Illinois, 9

Kinsey, Alfred, 6

marriage rights, 14, 20, 23
Maryland, 14
Massachusetts, 20
Matthew Shepard Act, 18, 20

New York, 10–11, 12
New York City Museum of Modern Art, 15

Obama, Barack, 15

Pennsylvania, 9
#Pride, 4, 15, 20, 27
pro-LGBTQ laws, 9, 18, 20, 23

Rodwell, Craig, 12

San Francisco Gay Freedom Day Parade, 14
Schoonmaker, Craig L., 12
Shepard, Matthew, 18, 20
social media, 4, 20, 23, 27
Society for Human Rights, 6
Stonewall Riots, 4, 10–11, 12, 23

Trump, Donald, 26

US military, 9, 14, 23, 26
US Supreme Court, 20, 23

Vermont, 20

White House, 15
Wyoming, 18